GAME DAY

GET READY FOR A SOCCER MATCH

by Emma Carlson Berne

Consultant: Beth Gambro
Reading Specialist, Yorkville, Illinois

Minneapolis, Minnesota

Teaching Tips

Before Reading

- Look at the cover of the book. Discuss the picture and the title.
- Ask readers to brainstorm a list of what they already know about soccer games. What can they expect to see in this book?
- Go on a picture walk, looking through the pictures to discuss vocabulary and make predictions about the text.

During Reading

- Read for purpose. Encourage readers to think about preparing for a soccer match as they are reading.
- Ask readers to look for the details of the book. What needs to happen before the big game?
- If readers encounter an unknown word, ask them to look at the sounds in the word. Then, ask them to look at the rest of the page. Are there any clues to help them understand?

After Reading

- Encourage readers to pick a buddy and reread the book together.
- Ask readers to name two things from the book that a player does to get ready for a soccer match. Find the pages that tell about these things.
- Ask readers to write or draw something they learned about soccer.

Credits:
Cover and title page, © I T A L O/Shutterstock and © QinJin/Shutterstock; 3, © kdshutterman/iStock; 5, © AzmanJaka/iStock; 7, © SDI Productions/iStock; 8–9, © Ridofranz/iStock; 11, © PeopleImages/iStock; 13, © Hero Images/iStock; 15, © PeopleImages.com - Yuri A/Shutterstock; 17, © FatCamera/iStock; 18–19, © matimix/iStock; 21, © nirat/iStock; 22T, © Marcus Lindstrom/iStock; 22M, © MesquitaFMS/iStock; 22B, © SolStock/iStock; 23TL, © DragonImages/iStock; 23TM, © wundervisuals/iStock; 23TR, © Rtimages/iStock; 23BL, © franckreporter/iStock; 23BM, © Lucky Dragon USA/Adobe Stock; and 23BR, © kali9/iStock.

Library of Congress Cataloging-in-Publication Data

Names: Berne, Emma Carlson, 1979- author.
Title: Get ready for a soccer match / by Emma Carlson Berne.
Description: Minneapolis, Minnesota : Bearport Publishing Company, [2024] |
  Series: Game day | Includes bibliographical references and index.
Identifiers: LCCN 2023002678 (print) | LCCN 2023002679 (ebook) | ISBN
  9798888220542 (library binding) | ISBN 9798888222508 (paperback) | ISBN
  9798888223697 (ebook)
Subjects: LCSH: Soccer--Juvenile literature. | Soccer players--Juvenile
  literature.
Classification: LCC GV943.25 .B47 2024 (print) | LCC GV943.25 (ebook) |
  DDC 796.334--dc23/eng/20230126
LC record available at https://lccn.loc.gov/2023002678
LC ebook record available at https://lccn.loc.gov/2023002679

Copyright © 2024 Bearport Publishing Company. All rights reserved. No part of this publication may be reproduced in whole or in part, stored in any retrieval system, or transmitted in any form or by any means, electronic, mechanical, photocopying, recording, or otherwise, without written permission from the publisher.

For more information, write to Bearport Publishing, 5357 Penn Avenue South, Minneapolis, MN 55419.

Contents

Let's Play! 4

How to Play 22
Glossary 23
Index 24
Read More 24
Learn More Online 24
About the Author 24

Let's Play!

Thwack!

The ball flies toward the goal.

It is time to play soccer.

Tomorrow is game day.

I am ready!

My **coach** showed me how to kick and pass.

I learned how to shoot a goal.

I will need lots of energy for the game.

So, I go to bed on time.

I wake up feeling rested.

It is time for a healthy breakfast.

I eat eggs and toast.

Then, I drink a big glass of water.

Next, I put on my **gear**.

My team wears red.

I pull on my socks and **shin guards**.

Next, I lace up my **cleats**.

When I get to the field, I do some **stretches**.

I touch my toes.

And I reach my arms out.

I also twist from side to side.

Time for warm-ups with the team!

Jogging gets our **muscles** going.

We kick the ball back and forth.

The game starts.

Go, team!

I cheer for everyone on the field.

They are all trying their best.

Soon, it is my turn.

I pass the ball to my friend.

He shoots.

Score!

I love soccer!

How to Play

A soccer match starts at the center of the field. Each team tries to score in the goals. These are at the ends of the field.

Most players can use any body part but their arms or hands to move the ball.

Each team has a goalie. They try to stop the ball from getting in the goal. They can use their hands.

Glossary

cleats shoes with bumps on the bottom for gripping the ground

coach the person who teaches and leads a sports team

gear things to wear and use for an activity

muscles parts of the body that help us move

shin guards pads worn to keep the front of the legs safe

stretches ways of moving the body to pull muscles longer

Index

bed 8
breakfast 10
cheer 18
coach 6
gear 12
goal 4, 6, 22
stretches 14
warm-ups 16

Read More

Leed, Percy. *Soccer: A First Look (Read about Sports).* Minneapolis: Lerner Publications, 2023.

Rose, Rachel. *Megan Rapinoe: Soccer Superstar (Bearcub Bios).* Minneapolis: Bearport Publishing Company, 2021.

Learn More Online

1. Go to **www.factsurfer.com** or scan the QR code below.
2. Enter "**Soccer Match**" into the search box.
3. Click on the cover of this book to see a list of websites.

About the Author

Emma Carlson Berne lives with her family in Cincinnati, Ohio. Horseback riding is her favorite sport.